The NOW Coloring Book | Guided Meditations for Stress Relief and Healing

I hope that this book will bring comfort to all people, but especially those who are coping with physical or mental illnesses. So first and foremost, I dedicate this book to anyone who is looking to find a bit of peace and comfort. To you I say, "Peace be with you!" and I hope that you enjoy the present moment. My prayer is for you to find grace, peace, and joy.

Secondly, I thank God for all the good things in my life, and that includes this book. I've been around the block a few times, and I can honestly say that I wouldn't be here if it were not for Jesus. He made me strong when I was at my weakest in life. He is my guide, my hope, and my Lord, and I'm just so thankful to serve a God who loves like He does. I hope that through this book, I can share that love with others.
- Tom

Tom keep up the good work!
Thank you God, my wife Neyda, my two kids Ariana and Giancarlo and to all my family.
- Arody

For more please visit us online at www.hopeincolor.com

Follow us on: recoverycoloringbook  @color4fun

_____

COPYRIGHT © 2016 by Recovery Coloring Books, LLC.
All rights reserved by Recovery Coloring Books, LLC.

No part of this publication may be reproduced in whole or in part, or stored in a retrieval system, or transmitted in any form or by any means, electronic, mechanical, photocopying, recording, or otherwise, without written permission of the publisher.

ISBN: 978-0-9962817-2-0
First Edition. Feb., 2016

The NOW Coloring Book

Guided Meditations for Stress Relief and Healing

By
Tom Castelloe

Illustrated by
Arody J. Victoria

Introduction:

I've called this *The Now Coloring Book* because it's designed to help you be present. Its goal is to aid you in celebrating the current moment, the "now," as a great gift from God, our creator. In my own life, I've found that coloring is an excellent way to be present and to fill myself with a simple joy. It's helped me to release stress and anxiety and to make my life better. This book combines coloring with meditation: two powerful practices that I firmly believe can help anyone find peace and joy.

Don't worry if you're not very experienced with meditation or coloring. This book is designed to be easy for anyone to use. Worried that you're not very creative? Don't be. This coloring book is just for you, and no one will judge your drawings. You don't have to be an artist; you just have to be willing to have some fun. Worried that you won't be able to meditate? You don't have to be an expert to try it. If you can sit and think, you can use this book. In fact, the pairing of coloring and meditating is meant to make meditating easier. The first time I tried to meditate, I couldn't focus. But when I tried coloring, I found that it was easy to get into a calm, almost blank state of mind. I was fully in the present. That's what gave me the idea for this book.

In recent years, psychologists have begun describing coloring as an alternative form of meditation, one that can have wide-ranging mental health benefits. The simple, repetitive action of coloring brings you into the present and creates a calm space that reduces stress and anxiety. It recreates the simple joy of childhood and helps to unlock your creativity. It helps you to subconsciously process feelings and worries. In essence, you can use coloring as a kind of active meditation.

This book pairs beautiful designs with simple meditations in the form of guided imagery. Each meditation asks you to imagine something, think of something, or do something. They are all simple and easy to follow. Each meditation has something in common: they help you to focus on the "now." When you use this book, I want you to use it as a break from worrying about the past or the future. Instead, allow yourself to rest in the present moment. Each meditation is also designed to leave you full of positive feelings: calm, peace, joy, thankfulness, and love.

The way that you use this book is up to you. You may want to work coloring into your routine. Set aside a time each day when you color and meditate as a way to find calm. Or, use this book when you need it. When you feel yourself overwhelmed or stressed, help yourself by meditating. You can flip through the book and find a title that speaks to you: what do you need? What are you struggling with? You might find an answer on the page in front of you.

On each page, I recommend that you start by reading through the guided meditation. Take some time to dwell on it and let it sink in. Then, as you color, continue to think about the meditation passage. You might start to focus on things like the color and design, and that's fine. If you find your mind straying to things like errands or everyday worries, gently bring yourself back to the meditation passage. Feel free to go back and forth between coloring and concentrating on the guided meditation. You may choose to spend a lot of time just processing the meditation, or you might find that it works better to think about it as you color. Find what works best for you.

Each meditation passage is accompanied by a "saying to repeat." This is a short phrase you can repeat either aloud or in your head as you color. It should help you to focus and to affirm the passage's core meaning. These sayings are also designed to be easy to remember. Feel free to use them in your everyday life. When you find yourself getting stressed or angry, you can repeat one of the calming sayings to yourself. It should remind you of how you felt as you meditated so that you can find your inner peace. This might not come naturally at first, but the more you practice it, the better you'll get.

Remember that this book is yours, and you can use it in whichever way helps you to find peace and happiness. You can cut out the designs to tape up in your room or office so that you have a touch of calm wherever you are. Or keep the book private, as you might keep a journal. You may want to go through the designs in order, or flip around and find what speaks to you. However you use it, I hope that it helps you to find joy and to feel the presence of God.

Meditation 1

Be Here Now

Take a moment just to be. Allow yourself to be fully present in the now. Too often, we focus on the past and the future and lose out on the present. For one moment, enjoy simply existing in the right now. Experience the present by letting go of plans, worries, and memories. Pay attention to your breath going in and out, and spread your consciousness out through your body.

SAYINGS TO REPEAT:

"Now is enough," and "I am fully present in this moment."

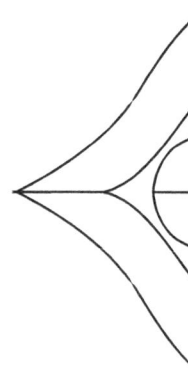

Meditation 2

Let Go of Tension

Let go of tension that has gathered in your mind and body. Imagine your body being full of water, and then let that water drain out. Start with your head and move down through your neck, shoulders, arms, torso, hips, legs, and feet. Release any muscles that you are holding tense. Allow your body to visibly relax, and picture warm water pouring out over your body. When you are done, you should feel loose and weightless. Picture yourself as a swan gliding effortlessly over a lake.

SAYINGS TO REPEAT:
"Tension drains out of me," and "I am weightless."

Meditation 3

Enjoy Each Breath

We don't often think about breathing, but every breath is a precious gift to you from our maker. Each breath is a sign that you are alive, enjoying the air of this world and drawing breath into strong lungs. Practice being thankful for this gift and the many others you have. Appreciate each breath as you breathe in and out. Notice how every breath is unique; just as no two snowflakes or no two flowers are identical, no two breaths are exactly the same. Relax while you enjoy each breath and color in the flowers.

SAYINGS TO REPEAT:

"This breath is a gift," and "I am thankful."

Meditation 4

Find Calm

Life can throw all kinds of turbulence at us, but we all have the ability to find calm at our center. Breathe deeply and work on finding a seed of calm, then let it spread. Create a mental list of things that make you feel calm and peaceful: things like fixing tea, listening to classical music, or going for a walk. Imagine yourself doing these things. Let yourself relax into calmness.

SAYINGS TO REPEAT:

"I have calm in me," and "I am calm."

Meditation 5

Be at Peace with Yourself

Take a moment to be at peace with yourself and with the world. Remember that you were placed into this world, and you belong in it. Your personhood is a gift. Even if there are things you want to change, assure yourself that you are on the right path and that everything will be fine. Feel peace echoing within yourself and emanating out from you. Just like a dove, you are a center of peace.

SAYING TO REPEAT: "Peace, peace, peace."

Meditation 6

Love Yourself

You deserve to be surrounded by love, including your love for yourself. No one is perfect, but remember that you are one of God's great creations. You have value, potential, and goodness inside you. Take a moment to recognize your own value, and respect yourself for who you are, not just what you do. If you need to, forgive yourself for mistakes. Learn to love yourself, and you can carry that love with you everywhere you go. You are like a bright sun. Your light can illuminate yourself and those around you.

SAYINGS TO REPEAT: "I'm learning to love myself and that's a good thing," and "I have value."

Meditation 7

Share Your Gifts

One of the easiest ways to make a bad day better is to give to someone else. Recognize that you have wonderful gifts to share with the world, whether it's a talent, a professional skill, or the warmth of your personality. Make a point to share a gift with someone else. That could mean a physical gift, like a piece of artwork that you make, or an emotional gift such as a smile or comforting words. Find the ways you have been blessed and then spread those out into the world. You may be amazed by how wonderful it makes you feel.

SAYING TO REPEAT: "I have gifts to share."

Meditation 8

Give Thanks

If you are currently struggling, one of the best ways to find improvement is by practicing gratitude. It's easy to see negativity, especially when things are going wrong. Instead, make it a habit to recognize the positive things around you, and give thanks for those. Gratitude for life is important, and it will lift you up. Think of 10 things you are thankful for right now. You can start with simple things, such as a hot cup of coffee or a comfortable bed, or include big things, such as people you love and opportunities you have had.

SAYING TO REPEAT: *"I am thankful for…"*

Meditation 9

Take Time to Talk with God

Just as you take the time to talk with family and friends, put aside time to talk with God. Prayer is a direct conversation with God, a conversation that will nurture your spirit. It's important to take care of your spiritual side, and prayer is always available as a spiritual exercise. Share your feelings, fears, hopes, and thoughts with God aloud or silently. Trust that God will hear you and send help in His own way.

SAYINGS TO REPEAT:

"God can hear me," and "I am connected to God."

Meditation 10

Test Your Dexterity

Try coloring with your non-dominant hand. Don't be critical of yourself; open yourself up to doing something different, and to being uncomfortable trying something new. You may feel like a kid who's first learning to write. Feel free to laugh and enjoy the freedom of having no expectations for yourself. We can find wisdom and personal growth when we try something from the beginning.

SAYINGS TO REPEAT:

"I give myself permission to fail," and "I don't need perfection."

Meditation 11

Let Go of a Lion's Roar!

Sometimes we need a simple release to get rid of tension and pent-up emotions. So let go of a lion's roar! Open your mouth and eyes wide, and give out a loud roar. You'll get rid of any tension you're holding in your face and chest. You may want to roar a couple of times until you stop feeling silly and start feeling confident. Roar until you feel strong!

SAYING TO REPEAT: "ROAR!"

Meditation 12

Breathe Out

Use your breathing to let go of stress, worries, and tension. First, make yourself comfortable. Take off or adjust uncomfortable clothing items, and sit or stand in a relaxing position. If your hair is up, let it down so it can fall around you freely. Your goal is to feel comfortable and uninhibited. Then inhale deeply, and let out a big sigh. Feel free to make an audible sigh, filled with your feelings and worries of the day. Repeat deep breathing, and each time you exhale, picture all of your stress leaving your body. With each breath, you should feel more calm, relaxed, and peaceful.

SAYINGS TO REPEAT:

"I breathe out stress," and "In and out" (as you breathe).

Meditation 13

Visit Your Joyful Place

Think of a time or a place where you felt happy, joyful, and content. Maybe it was a beach vacation, a secret place in your childhood home, or a happy day spent with family and friends. Visit the place in your mind, and imagine all the details that make it real: the way it looked, sounded, and smelled. Remember all the details that made that place so happy. What about being there made you feel relaxed and content? Recreating this place can provide you with a place of happy respite in your mind. Hold onto the image until you feel a sense of happiness spreading through you.

SAYINGS TO REPEAT:

"I am in my joyful place," and "I am filled with joy."

Meditation 14

Picture Your Dreams Coming True

Visualization is powerful, and your dreams are powerful. Choose a dream that's important to you right now, and visualize it coming true. It can be a big or a small dream: driving in a new car, getting a promotion, finishing a degree, making the perfect cup of coffee, spending time with someone important to you, and so on. Picture yourself accomplishing that goal, and think about how that accomplishment will make you feel. Believe that you can reach your goals, and never let go of your dreams.

SAYINGS TO REPEAT:

"My dreams are within reach," and "I can make my dreams come true."

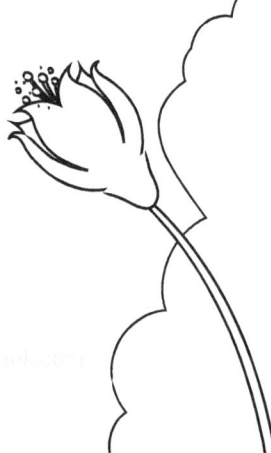

Meditation 15

Play Fort

Imagine building a simple fort out of sheets, cardboard boxes, and pillows as a kid. Remember the feeling of pride and contentment you felt as you sat in that fort. Think about a place in your home that can have that same feeling of safety and joy. What makes a space your own? Is it pictures on the wall, or decorations that you've picked out? Imagine a space that is perfectly your own.

SAYING TO REPEAT: "I am at home here."

Meditation 16

Release a Great Big Yawn

Yawning is a natural response to feeling tired, and it provides your body with an influx of oxygen. Yawning is a great way to help you relax. Give a big, exaggerated, out loud yawn. Feel free to stretch out your arms as you do it. Then try yawning a few more times. Yawning is contagious, so it will be easy to give a real yawn after the first one. Then, breathe deeply. You'll be processing a lot of oxygen and carbon dioxide, and you'll feel more relaxed.

SAYING TO REPEAT: "Relax, relax."

Meditation 17

Pick Out a Color

Choose a colored pencil or pen. Why did you choose that color? What does this color mean to you? What does it remind you of or make you feel? Start drawing, and pay attention to how the color looks on paper. Is it dark or bright? What about its texture? Colors are around us all day, but we rarely think about them. One part of coloring is paying attention to simple but beautiful details. For a moment now, fully absorb this single color and what it means to you.

SAYING TO REPEAT:

The name of the color e.g. "Blue, blue."

Meditation 18

Smile More

The simple act of smiling can lift your mood and give happiness to others. Even if you don't feel like it right now, practice smiling. Research shows that smiling communicates to the brain that we are content and calm. It may not come easily at first, but try your best. Think of things that make you smile: a happy memory, a funny joke, a silly moment. Work on making your smile as genuine as possible, and you may be surprised by how it changes your mood for the better. A smile reminds you that you have power over your own happiness.

SAYINGS TO REPEAT:
"I feel a smile coming on," "The whole world smiles with me," and "I have the power to improve my mood."

Meditation 19

Be Weightless

Sometimes it can feel as if our troubles and worries are weighing us down. Visualize yourself letting go of all your struggles and stressors. Imagine each worry as a burden you are carrying, and lay each one down in turn. Feel as the weight lifts off you; feel as your back gets a little straighter with each burden you cast off. You have stripped yourself of all your weights and burdens. Now picture yourself stepping into a warm ocean and floating on top of the water. You are weightless and free, gently and effortlessly supported.

SAYINGS TO REPEAT:

"I am weightless," and "I am free of my troubles."

Meditation 20

Celebrate Your Creative Self

If you are using this book, you have a creative side! Appreciate your creativity and your ability to create. Flip back through this book, and look at the drawings you've completed. Take pride in your use of colors and your vision. Think of how you are building your creativity, and how you can use that creativity to release positivity into the world. Celebrate yourself, and be proud of your creativity!

SAYINGS TO REPEAT:
"I am creative," and "I have a creative self that makes a difference in this world."

Meditation 21

Affirmations Can Make a Difference

Saying things out loud affects the way you think. Try saying something good about yourself right now. Repeat it until you really feel it in your heart. It's okay if you feel silly at first, just keep trying. Is there something you're worried about right now? Repeat to yourself that you can do it, or that it will be fine. Affirming is a first step to believing, and believing is the first step to accomplishing. Just like a peacock shows off its beautiful feathers, you can affirm positive things about yourself.

SAYINGS TO REPEAT:

"I am a good person," "I love myself," and "I am strong."

Meditation 22

Take Note of Your Body in Space

As you color in this drawing, try to be fully present in the moment. Spread out your awareness to feel your body in space. How do your back and legs feel against the chair? How does the pencil or marker feel in your hand? How does the air feel against your face? Are you holding any tension in your body? Let yourself be aware of it. Just as you color this cat stretching out, let your mind feel out your body as it exists in space.

SAYINGS TO REPEAT:

"I am aware of my body," and "My body and mind are one."

Meditation 23

Breathe Deeply and Purposefully

Slowing your breathing can help you to feel relaxed and centered. Breathe in to a count of 5. Pause for 3-5 seconds, and then breathe out to a count of 8. Repeat until you feel relaxed. Picture gentle waves moving in and out at the beach, just like your breath. Waves move constantly, keeping the ocean vibrant and bringing life to the shore. Waves leave beautiful patterns in the sand, and they can leave behind lines of pebbles and sea shells. As you color in this seashell design, continue to breathe slowly and to think of yourself as a calm ocean, with waves going in and out.

SAYINGS TO REPEAT:

"I am calm like the sea," and "Breaths moving in and out."

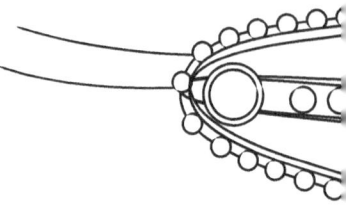

Meditation 24

Connect with Your Inner Rhythm

Life is full of business and chaos, which can make you feel off balance. Take a moment to stop moving and be still. Sit calmly, and allow yourself to find a balanced stillness. Instead of forcing your limbs not to move, allow them to relax into calm. Focus on the inside of yourself. You'll notice that your body contains constant movement and sound: the beating of your heart, the flow of blood, the drawing of breath. You contain a constant, calm rhythm. Listen to this rhythm for a minute until you feel in synch with it. Remember that wherever you go, whatever you do, this rhythm remains steadily beating inside of you. You can always reconnect with it.

SAYINGS TO REPEAT:

"I feel the beat inside of me," and "I create my own rhythm."

Meditation 25

God is Love

God loves you perfectly and unconditionally. That love can comfort and inspire you if you open yourself up to it. Close your eyes, and feel God's love within you. It is a light that can warm you and give you hope even in the darkest of times. Allow God's love to spread through you, and you can share that love with others as well.

SAYINGS TO REPEAT:

"I am loved," and "God loves me."

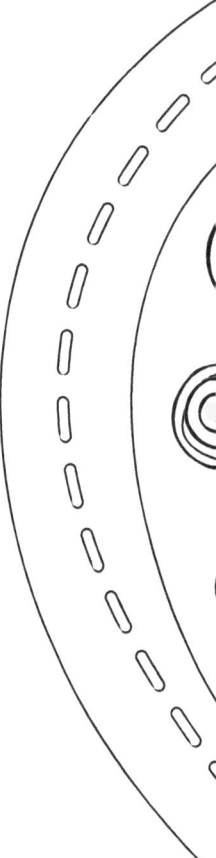
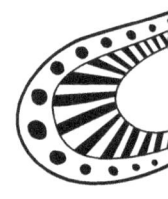

Meditation 26

Try Progressive Muscle Relaxation

Progressive muscle relaxation is a technique through which you focus on and relax each part of your body. Using it, you can find tension that you weren't aware of and loosen up your entire body. Follow these steps, and then try to maintain your relaxation as you color.
Concentrate on your feet. Tighten your feet muscles for a few seconds. And release.
Concentrate on your lower legs. Tighten and release.
Concentrate on your thighs. Tighten and release.
Concentrate on your abdomen. Tighten and release.
Concentrate on your chest. Tighten and release.
Concentrate on your back. Tighten and release.
Concentrate on your hands/fists. Tighten and release.
Concentrate on your arms. Tighten and release.
Concentrate on your neck. Tighten and release.
Concentrate on your face. Tighten and release.
Take a slow, deep breath and settle in to relaxation after concentrating on your muscles.

SAYINGS TO REPEAT:

"Tighten and release," and "Letting go of tension."

Meditation 27

Connect with Your Inner Child

Take a moment to connect with your inner child. Remember how as a child, you could live totally in the moment without any worries. Think about games you used to play and the simple joy you felt. Think about how imagination and silliness used to fill your days. Now, bring the joy of playfulness and the happiness of simply being back into the present. Remember how investigating nature used to be a joy — something as simple as observing a lady bug on a flower. How can you incorporate the spirit of playfulness into adulthood? Remind yourself that simple happiness is not immature; it's wise. You deserve pure joy.

SAYINGS TO REPEAT:
"Happiness is mine to enjoy," "The child within me is loveable," and "I deserve joy."

Meditation 28

Celebrate "The Good Fruits"

Just as you would collect a fruit harvest, harvest the fruits of the spirit that the Bible tells us about: love, joy, peace, forbearance, kindness, goodness, faithfulness, gentleness, and self-control. These fruits will provide your soul with nourishment and strength. Hold them close to you, and nurture them to help them grow. They will help you be the best version of yourself, and they will bring happiness to you and those around you.

SAYING TO REPEAT:

"I am blessed with bountiful fruits."

Meditation 29

Laughter is Good for You

Research suggests that joyful laughter and meditation have similar effects on the brain. Laughter is an excellent tool to help you cope with painful or uncomfortable feelings. Both laughter and meditation will change your mind for the better, leaving you feeling calmer and more at ease. Have you ever noticed that after a hearty laugh, you feel as if you've let go of the pent-up tension of negative feelings? That's because laughter is an emotional release. Right now, let out a laugh. It's okay if it feels forced at first. You can think of a funny memory or joke to help. Remember that the more you laugh, the better your mood will become. Make a commitment to laughing more often every day, and you'll add more brightness to your life.

SAYINGS TO REPEAT:

"Laughter is bubbling up," and "Hohoho hehehe hahaha."

Meditation 30

Share Your Love!

Love is a wonderful thing, and it only becomes more beautiful as you share it. Sometimes it feels like sharing love opens us up to being hurt, or drains us of a precious resource, but this isn't always true. Love is unending, and you don't limit your supply of love by sharing it. Instead, you strengthen your love. Each time you share your love with someone else, you bless them with a great gift. Think about ways you have already released your love into the world. How did it make you feel to see others blessed by your love? How can you release love in the future? Remember that you can share love in ways big and small. The best thing is that the more you let love out to others, the more you see love in the world all around you. The more you share love, the more it grows and surrounds you.

SAYINGS TO REPEAT:

"I have love to share," and "My love is plentiful."

www.ingramcontent.com/pod-product-compliance
Lightning Source LLC
Chambersburg PA
CBHW082224010526
44113CB00037B/2521